Radical Release

*Breaking Away from Bondage to a
Life of Freedom — God's Way*

GLORIA POAGE

NEWMAN SPRINGS PUBLISHING
320 Broad Street
Red Bank, NJ 07701

First originally published by Newman Springs Publishing 2019

All scriptures taken from King James Version of the bible.

ISBN 978-1-64096-958-2 (Paperback)
ISBN 978-1-64096-959-9 (Digital)

Printed in the United States of America

Contents

Acknowledgments

Thank you
Nancy Simmons
for the many hours of editing.
Without you, this book would not have happened.

And
To Dr. Dawn Forbes
Your encouragement led to turning the *Radical Release* transcript into a book.

To both of you
I am forever grateful.

Introduction

Two things of certainty are set in stone—life and death. Once a birth takes place, there is no going back. That life proceeds through a variety of influences which mold it to its eventual culmination.

The purpose of this book is to present life's truth to you, the reader, the kind of truth that will make you free. You indeed will receive the opportunity and privilege of examining your life and its purpose to the end of radically releasing yourself into making conscious decisions that will be of great value to your spiritual well-being.

In reading, no doubt you will become overwhelmed at times. However, persevere, as you will be a stronger person when you face life with soberness and sincerity, maybe for the first time. The goal is to attain personal freedom and success, rather than bondage with unanswered questions. A solution exists to every problem, and you gain fulfillment when answers come and problems are solved to a satisfactory conclusion. Hopefully, this book will point you in the direction that will do just that. The intent is that peace, joy, and freedom will invade you as your eyes open to a world of victory in overcoming the issues of life that make you less than the person you desire to be.

Whether you're on top of the world today or whether the world is on top of you, this book will bring freshness to your spirit, soul, and body that will thrill your very heart.

Choices

For thousands of years, men and women have lived and made history, but they are now dead and gone. Gone where? Webster's Dictionary defines "gone" as the past participle of go. Go means to move along, proceed, or move to a particular place. Yet, when a person dies, he is dead, isn't he? He is useless compared to when he lived!

Let's talk about when he lived. That living body was driven by something that made him move. Every living and functioning human being has a brain that affords him intellect, feelings, emotions, energy, and every other description of life. When life resides inside us, we move.

In the present era most people move along in life preoccupied with day-to-day survival. They give little serious attention to where they'll be next week, next month, next year, or a thousand years from now. Some wise person said that "There was a time when you were not, but there will never be a time when you are not." This saying means that from conception, you will forever live. So the real you is not simply your body. Your body is just the house in which the real you live.

Where is this going? Yes, you agree that you have a mind that operates within your brain which prompts your body to act and

9

react. Animals do the same thing. But what makes you different from animals? We all know that humans can dominate everything else in creation. Humans are set apart with a spirit, however, that an animal does not have. This spirit is the innermost self that divinely resides within your being. It is intertwined with your mind and emotions. This spirit is the real you, and it is unique to everyone who has ever lived or ever will live. Although animals do have a soul(ish) nature—mind and emotions—they do not have a divine spirit.

The five senses receive much attention: what we see, taste, hear, smell, or feel. These senses are important to our daily living but have little effect on the spirit. Although we cannot see the spirit physically, it is the forever part of us. So shouldn't your spirit, which is the real you, be given more attention than the body (physical) or even the mind (the emotional and thinking part of mankind)? Before the time when your spirit moves out of your body, it would be very sensible to discover to where this spirit will be moving, as this is the real and the forever you.

Since we are into the forever part of mankind (the spirit), then we must discover what the greater Spirit orchestrated us to be who we are, embodied in a frame or house called the human body. History illustrates that mankind's survival on this earth has occurred with a great deal of help from outside forces. Throughout the ages many who were up against odds impossible to humanly overcome have witnessed unexplainable miracles. Whether or not we choose to believe it, a higher source is in absolute charge and control. The Holy Bible describes Him in great detail.

Some might say they don't believe the Bible. If you are one of them, have you personally read it for yourself? For centuries unbelievers have launched campaigns to disprove the Holy Bible and the existence of God, only to discover in the course of study a God of love who is beyond everything they could speak or think.

The Bible has stood the test of time. That is the sure proof of truth. The Bible is a complete work that details a three-dimensional portrait of God, as well as a portrait of everything about us, His greatest creation. The Holy Bible states flatly that "forever success" occurs only when we, His human creation, on an individual basis, come to the realization that God is our Maker and it is through Him and His sacrificial provision that we have hope in this life and the absolute assurance of heaven when the life moves out of our body.

Whether you believe the Holy Bible or not, this is your opportunity to confirm your belief. Opportunities present themselves to us at unpredictable times in life and at most needful times. Circumstances evolve, and consequences result—every time. However it happened that you came to the point of holding this book in your hands, it happened not by accident. Yet, this book holds no magic. It contains nothing new that has not been said before. This is merely your time to stop and privately take a look at your life and where you are going. Don't be intimidated by fear of the unknown. The unknown is simply the known not investigated.

This book sets forth no religion. It is not about a religion at all. It is about a discovery that will insure your eternity in a good place. Heaven is that place. The very word is uplifting to the spirit of man. Search out your future. By doing so, you will have made a genuine decision that is a life-or-death choice.

Do you believe in God? Do you believe within your innermost self that there is One who created you and that this same One created the world and everything in it? Scores of people believe that some force greater than themselves must have created everything; but, apart from that, they have never pursued the thought further.

Consider nature. Untouched by human hands, nature is beautiful. It reaches up and out to light. It presents everything it has for the taking. Nature gives itself to be possessed, admired, studied, and even mutilated. The One who made it has given it to us as a gift. Hard to believe? Read on.

Nature is given freely to all. But, no matter how much we appreciate, adore, or abhor anything we experience with our five senses, we have our limited view of it. Our minds can take in but a small cube of any one thing. And when we think we understand any one thing, that one thing is so clouded by our particular worldview that we can hardly find another person to agree on our full understanding of it.

This world and everything in it, down to every single molecule, are so complex, minutely detailed, and huge in its scope that one would be an absolute fool to deny that there is a God who made it and is in control of it all. The order of God's creation is simple, but when we delve into how it works, it becomes mind-boggling.

It takes only a small degree of intelligence to realize that no matter how much or little we know, it is only a drop in the ocean to the knowledge that is available. When we look at it that way, it could be depressing because suddenly we become aware of how very small we are in this world and how smitten with limitations we are. Yet, look at the big picture. Everything still moves along with great order—the sun and moon still rise and set daily, yielding twenty-four-hour cycles of opportunity.

God *is* God, as is so clearly stated in the Bible; and we humans are His highest creation, created in His image *(Genesis 1:27)*. He is God because He spoke everything into existence and then molded the first man from the dust of the earth; after which, procreation proceeded in God's design. We have the capacity to have God's character because at our birth it was His breath that was breathed into us that made us living creatures. God gave us our first gift at birth—the gift of breathing! Everything, from our very breath to the magnitude of the universe itself, has been designed with wisdom so vast that we learn to receive and use what we need of it with little or no consideration of Who is behind it all.

We are not to know everything; otherwise, we would be tempted to think we could replace God. In Scripture, God calls Himself Father, and He refers to us as His children. Everything in the natural realm is a symbol of the spiritual. Natural fathers know more than their children as God the Father knows more than we, His children, do. Children of a good father accept the fact that the father knows more. They are therefore open to his instructions.

God is huge in the scope of our being. He gives us our very life. He is unlimited. He has given us a plan which we learn by reading and studying one small book, the Holy Bible. If we stop to think about it, God shows us how limited we are in our finite abilities by giving us such a small book of instruction to read and study. History is full of scores of smart men who have given their lives to reading and studying it and modeling their existence on its principles. It makes good sense to examine the Bible to the fullest because what it says is without error. It describes mankind's nature, both physical and spiritual, to the fullest. Our eternity, whether we spend it in heaven or hell, hinges on how we respond to what is written in His Holy Word. He *is* God, and we can trust Him.

But you say, "I don't know what to do with this! I don't know what I believe. I'm confused, and it frustrates me to think of all this spiritual 'stuff.'" At this point, you don't know whether to laugh at the idea or to be scared. You must admit, however, that you and you alone must handle the responsibility for the real issues in your life. It is personal. If God is real and the Bible true, you must discover the truth of it for yourself. If heaven and hell are real, it makes sobering sense to search and decide for yourself where you will be spending your forever when your spirit moves from your body.

As the mother eagle pushes the eaglet out of the nest, the frightening rush must be heartrending for the small bird. The eaglet, in its descent, flaps its wings in desperation without hope in its downward fall to certain death until the mother rescues the baby bird and carries it back to the nest. This example is a picture of what you will experi-

13

ence as you leap into the unknown, suddenly to discover that you are being carried from a life of uncertainty to one of vision and victory, one that allows you to enjoy living as God intended you to live.

This is your opportunity to make a decision. It is truly a matter of choice—life or death. As you launch into this pursuit for truth, your life will become one of expectancy filled with unexplainable adventure. Perhaps for the first time you will begin understanding that days lived in the trust of the Maker of the universe bring fulfillment; and this fulfillment evolves into a life that is truly worth living, not only in the here and now but in the world that is ahead of us all, in a world and life that will never end.

The Map

The creation story began over six thousand years ago and has been capsulated into one chapter, the first chapter of the first book of what we call the Bible, our life's Map. That book, Genesis, means beginning. Here again, God in his magnitude gives only a brief sketch or portrait of how He created everything. But can't man create as well? The difference is that God "spoke" the physical out of nothing. God spoke this universe into being. Man can create only if he has something already in existence with which to work. Man has tried to explain God's creation story in humanistic ways called theories, but to the serious student of the Spirit (God), man's explanations simply do not have merit.

It is amusing to read in the first chapter of Genesis simple statements outlining our beginnings. In Genesis 1:16, God states, almost as an afterthought, that He "made the stars also!" Think of the volumes of books researching the complexities of the stars and galaxies alone. With all of man's study and commentary on any one particle of creation, that study leads the student into even broader and endless horizons of exploration.

God is Spirit (*John 4:24*), and it was by the command of His Spirit and in His wisdom that all things came into existence. God is the God of order. We see that in the progressive steps of creation.

From darkness came light, then the heavens, dry land, the seas, plants and seeds yielding food, the sun and moon, fish and birds, and, finally, animals and human beings. The oversimplification of the creation account in Genesis is unbelievable to those who have not yet recognized and accepted that there is a God. The Bible calls them fools in Psalm 14:1. The fool puffs up his little chest and brags of his strength and mastery over his destiny, when the reality is that God, the master Designer, voluntarily gives him the gift of his very next involuntary heartbeat.

God was and is merciful and gracious in giving us the Bible. God put into the hearts of chosen men to state exactly what He intended mankind to receive, believe, and study.

2 Timothy 3:16–17 says that "All Scripture is given by inspiration of God, and is profitable for doctrine, for reproof, for correction, for instruction in righteousness, that the man of God may be complete, thoroughly equipped for every good work."

God presents Himself in Scripture in ways that a child can understand. He does not try to sell Himself to us, yet is relentless in offering an open invitation to know Him, to come into the knowledge of whom He is, and to learn His character. That is love! Although in absolute control of this world and everything in it, He allowed his first created beings, Adam and Eve, the freedom of choice. He gave them instruction that would keep them safe and in perfect harmony with Him, the God of the universe. The Garden of Eden was paradise given to them for their eternal pleasure. Their human weakness surfaced, however, when they chose to disobey God's instruction not to eat of the tree of the knowledge of good and evil.

We have the same choice today. If we choose God's way of instruction, we will each live a fulfilled life that leads to an understanding of God's purpose for our lives. But more often than not, mankind chooses his own way in disobedience to the will of God; and this disobedience leads to a greater knowledge of evil. When evil (sin) overwhelms us, we cry out to God who rescues us over again. That is love. Total love entrusts us with the freedom of choice. If God had given mankind only the freedom to choose the good, that would not have been an expression of total love. Pure love must be held with an open hand. When we begin to truly love and seek God, it will not be through His coercion that we become a part of His family; it will develop out of our own free will as we learn to trust and believe the words of the "Map" (the Bible). Learning the truths of the Map will become our greatest desire.

Throughout the Bible, God continually invites mankind to join Him. Isaiah 55:6 tells us to "Seek the Lord while He may be found, call upon Him while He is near." In verses 8–9, He tells us that His thoughts are not our thoughts, neither our ways His ways. He is so much higher than we are, but in His divine love, He knows about and concerns Himself with every detail of our individual lives. He tells us in verse 11 that His Word (the Bible) is spoken from His mouth and it will accomplish what He intends and it will prosper.

The following illustration parallels the advantages of following truth:

Imagine yourself as having built and being the head of a very large company. You would hope that every person working within your empire would know that all decisions you make would be for the success of the company and for the good of all.

On the first day of employment, each employee receives a copy of the company manual which contains a comprehensive description of you and the specific guidelines they must follow in order to guarantee their success in the organization. The lowest-skilled person in the empire could ultimately become one of your most successful employees by simply reading, understanding, and applying the principles set out in the manual. You would hope that every employee would trust the company manual of operation and be loyal and accepting of it in its entirety. Yet, from the vantage point of those on various levels within the empire, the manual might be perceived in a number of ways. Some might not read it at all. Some might casually read it. Some will read and apply the steps for success, thereby being promoted. The less workers read and apply the steps of the manual, the greater the danger for misunderstandings and confusion.

It comes down to the fact that you as the head of the company know the steps that insure your business' success. You know in your God-given wisdom that the company will succeed. Everyone in the organization has the invitation from you to get onboard for the benefit of the company. It is their choice as to whether or not they will comply. The choice is simple—either read and apply the principles of the manual for advancement or ignore them and fail.

This is an exact comparison to God, the Bible, and us, His human creation. God is ruling whether or not we comply. He is the Victor because His leadership is supreme. Just as He used certain men to provide us the Bible (our life's Map), He will insure that His plan succeeds.

In Luke 19:40, Jesus says that if His messengers did not speak out for Him, "the stones would immediately cry out." God has a plan; and mankind, nature, His angels, and other heavenly creations are helping Him carry it out. All will believe and acknowledge Him at one time or another whether we want to or not. We will not only acknowledge Him, but one day every knee will bow before Him *(Romans 14:11)*.

When asked, most people will say without hesitation that the Bible is truth. Songs and poetry point to it as our road to heaven. Biblical scholars speak assuredly that the Bible answers every question that could be asked. No matter what mankind speaks superficially, built within his nature is the fact that the Bible is a special book and one to be respected. Rather than just blindly acknowledging what others say, we need to make a conscious decision to investigate its truth as it applies to us individually.

18

Today we do not mean to dishonor God by ignoring the Bible. For most, it simply takes too much discipline to be quiet and still in this noisy world. Psalm 46:10 tells us to be still and know that He is God. When we become still and turn off the noise, we become awesomely aware that life is more than the physical here and now. When we add the Bible, God's Word, to that stillness, we discover another way of living. We soon realize that we are not in control as we once thought. It is challenging to our natures to accept that apart from God we are powerless. But as we immerse ourselves in the words of Scripture, our very inner fiber grows stronger; and we become aware of a protective shield that begins surrounding us, one that we've never before experienced. God shows us that for every design there must be a designer. Psalm 139:14 goes so far as to say that we are "fearfully and wonderfully made" and that we are marvelous creations.

When you develop a habit of reading the Bible, you will soon learn that you have a new life that is more powerful and victorious than anything else in this world. The Spirit of God will become your teacher. He will be your guide to lead you into a high calling unimaginable to your former thinking. No one will need to convince or prove to you the Bible's validity; you will experience it for yourself. Your only responsibility is to discover the real truth and pattern your life upon Him. It becomes a matter of life and death—life as God provides or death as we neglect to search out the truth. God *is* God, and His plan for mankind is specifically housed within the little book called the Bible.

As you begin investigating the Bible, many unanswered questions will arise. These questions will be infinite; answers will be also. That which you understand will be exciting and eye-opening. When answers do not come immediately, don't be discouraged or deceived into thinking that there are no solutions. At the most unexpected times, the answers will come. Just remember, although we understand very little about the intricacies of nature, our lack of understanding does not make them untrue. God reveals the mystery of His Word to each of us separately as it pertains to His individual plan for us.

2 Timothy 2:15 says to "Be diligent to present yourself approved to God, a worker who does not need to be ashamed, rightly dividing the word of truth." Once you understand the meaning of being approved of God, you will be in a position to go forward in a new life with Him. The spirit that God has placed in your body is the real you, and the real you will live forever in one of two places spelled out in the Map. This thought is radical, but, nevertheless, true.

The Great Divider

The first direct mention of Jesus in the Bible is in Genesis 1:26 when God said, "'Let Us' make man in 'Our' image." The prophet Isaiah wrote in detail about Him over seven hundred years before His birth when He proclaimed that a Child would be born, a Son given, and the very government would be on His shoulders (Isaiah 9:6). Isaiah identified Jesus as Wonderful, Counselor, Mighty God, Everlasting Father, and Prince of Peace, and that Jesus would establish His own government which would be one of everlasting peace.

Isaiah 53 describes Jesus as One coming to earth and being despised and rejected by mankind. It compares Jesus's crucifixion to that of a lamb brought to be slaughtered. He was the one and only perfect sacrifice required by Jehovah God. Why would God require that?

Before Adam and Eve sinned by their disobedience to God in the Garden of Eden, they were covered by the glory of God. Their nakedness was as innocent as that of a baby. However, after they sinned, their innocence fell away; and they became ashamed of their nakedness. Immediately, they tried to sew fig leaves together to cover themselves. To this day, mankind tries to conceal his sin shame in various ways. God, in His love and mercy, sacrificed the blood of animals and covered Adam and Eve with coats from those animal skins *(Genesis 3:21)*. From that original disobedience in the garden, a sin nature was born in Adam and Eve and in every offspring since. No longer did mankind reflect the image of God. Through Adam and Eve's act of disobedience, sin permeated the very fiber of humanity's nature. Through Christ, God then executed His eternal plan of restoring mankind to His standard of acceptance.

From the beginning, God required blood sacrifices for the forgiveness of sin. Blood represents life. As death came through sin, blood showed resurrection and life. Throughout the Old Testament, lambs, goats, cattle, and birds were slain and offered to God as sacrifices for atonement of sins. During those days, God spoke directly to and through the prophets of the Old Testament in order to communicate His law. Essentially His message was "be obedient and you will be blessed." The sin nature inbred into mankind was so strong, however, that in spite of all the blessings poured out on them, they invariably turned to their own ways of sin. Of course, God knew that mankind would never be strong enough on his own to overcome his sin nature. Therefore, throughout the Old Testament, God revealed His plan to send His sinless Son, the Messiah, to earth; and He would, once and for all, be offered as the absolute perfect sinless sacrifice.

Throughout the Old Testament era, God required that only the best of animals be sacrificed. This specification was a mirror image of the pure blood sacrifice that He would provide ultimately through Christ, His Son. Although the law of God required blood for the atonement of sin, animal sacrifices simply were not enough. Mankind's efforts to redeem were fruitless. For man to truly be redeemed, God Himself had to provide the sacrifice once for all, as nothing on earth could be totally freed of sin by the ritual of slaughtering animals. Man could make only feeble attempts to present himself right before a holy God. Adam and Eve gave mankind's perfect nature away when they sinned, thereby defiling the entire earth. Only God, Himself, could provide the required sacrifice for sin.

As was promised throughout scripture, God did provide His own sacrifice. This sacrifice was part of Him—Jesus Christ, His Son. Thousands of years passed from God's first sacrifice and covering Adam and Eve's sin to that final sacrifice of Jesus on the cross. That very window of time clearly shows the tenderness of a holy God in teaching us one step at a time truth that cannot be learned quickly. God is so very powerful, high, and holy that no human can look on Him. He is described in Deuteronomy 4:24 and Hebrews 12:29 as a "consuming fire." Yet, He made mankind in His own image and, from the time of creation, has sought to have a loving relationship with us. God is love. Love embraces. Love allows freedom. Love never forces.

Many ask the question, "If God is love, why does He allow suffering and bad things to happen on earth?" From the beginning, God allowed the freedom of choice. The Garden of Eden was heaven on earth for Adam and Eve. It was splendor. Yet, everything has two sides—light and dark, black and white, up and down, the tree of the knowledge of good and evil, etc. God gave Adam instruction to eat and enjoy the food of every tree except the tree of the knowledge of good and evil. Of all the good that surrounded them, Adam and Eve were lured and seduced into making a deadly mistake that brought separation from God. Being given the freedom of choice was an act of love. God had given fair warning of the consequences if they chose to disobey. God cannot and will not go back on His Word. Therefore, mankind's willful sin results in suffering and destruction.

God (Jesus) is the same yesterday, today, and forever (Hebrews 13:8). He gave Adam and Eve the freedom of choice in the Garden of Eden; and from the time of the original sin, mankind has gravitated to making wrong choices because of this innate sin nature. Yet, from the original sin, God made provision to restore mankind to a right relationship with Him. It was not by force. He offered one way, and that was by the sacrifice of blood. Ultimately, in the fullness of time, Jesus (God on earth) became the one and only acceptable sacrifice. Nothing or no one else could be offered because nothing or no one else was free of sin. Only the blood of a pure sacrifice could fully satisfy the requirement of a holy God. That purity was existent only within God Himself.

John 1:1 says that "In the beginning was the Word, and the Word was with God, and the Word was God." In verse 14, it is found "the Word became flesh and dwelt among us." The entire chapter of John 1 describes the Word as God's Son, Jesus. In verses 10–12 we are told that "He was in the world, and the world was made through Him, and the world did not know Him. He came to His own (the Jewish nation) and His own did not receive Him. But as many as received Him, to them He gave the right to become children of God, to those who believe in His name." God continues to give mankind choices.

Choices have consequences. Just as Adam and Eve were given the freedom of making choices, we continue to be given the same freedom. Our world is as good as it is because of a loving God who has made provision for us to live free. It is as bad as it is because mankind continues to make wrong choices and, in rebellion, has refused to accept the only sacrifice that will bring him back to all the good that God intended for him from the beginning.

From conception, every baby is unique. Built within the child are combinations of potential, but the miracle of this uniqueness is often overlooked. Generations come and go, but most never understand that all good things are gifts from a God who loves them. Some grow to identify their potential by gravitating to doing those things that come easy to them. As life continues, individuals often put so much attention on their gifts and talents, or lack thereof, that they never consider the Giver of the gifts and talents.

The more gifted we are, and because of our powerful sin natures, the greater danger we have of deifying our prideful selves and, in our fantasy, thinking we are the god of our destinies. In our freedom of choice, we can take the credit or blame for our lives, or we can give the credit or blame to Him. Whatever we do or think does not change the reality that God *is* God. Sin is sin, and we are plagued with it in this world. It is born in us. The only way we can be freed from it is in accepting the sacrifice that God Himself provided for us. That sacrifice is Jesus Christ, His Son. We have absolutely no other way to be accepted by Jehovah God.

Once we understand that God *is* God and He loves us and invites us, with all our strengths and weaknesses, to willingly give ourselves to a higher lifestyle, we then begin life as we were created to live. Our attention moves from perceiving that the world revolves around us, whether positively or negatively, to an awesome awareness that it is no longer about us but that it is all about a God who has a plan and desire to bring us into holiness that is far beyond what we can imagine. We begin to understand that God gave us our gifts and talents and we must develop and use them to His glory. He then blesses us with everything we can possibly desire. His blessing not only embraces this life but continues growing throughout eternity.

Jesus was that accepted sacrifice. He left heaven and entered the natural world through the physical body of a virgin girl. He was born and grew to manhood, pure and sinless, for thirty-three years on earth. Old Testament Jewish scholars knew that God would send a Messiah, but religion chose not to accept Jesus because He did not meet its expectations. He was royalty, but not the royalty the religious leaders wanted to see. Their pride blinded them from seeing the wisdom of why God would choose to physically enter this world through such humble beginnings. It was truly genius that the King of kings and the Lord of lords, Jesus, who is God in flesh, chose to enter this world through the lowliest of circumstances.

During His brief stay on earth, He forgave sin, healed the sick, raised the dead, and received whosoever would recognize Him as God. His message was "I am the way, the truth, and the life. No one comes to the Father except through Me" (John 14:6). Some saw the wisdom of it all and submitted themselves to Him. That invitation to submit and receive Him as the only sacrifice acceptable to a holy God continues today.

SUBMIT & RECEIVE HIM.

From the beginning of time, mankind has found it difficult to submit to a will other than his own. In their stout-hearted blindness, kings and leaders of the world continue to rebel against the Lord Jehovah and His anointed, Jesus. They attempt to break free from God and His way. The scripture says in Psalms 2:4 that "He who sits in the heavens shall laugh." There is no way to escape our loving God.

Every human being has a choice to make. God allows us that freedom of choice. Look at where you are right now. Can you see that God in heaven rules and that He requires only one thing of you that will free you in this earthly life as well as provide life with Him eternally? Jesus refers to Himself as the door to heaven in John 10:9. He says that if any man is to be saved, it will be through Him that we enter into salvation.

Jesus is the Divider, the truth, the door standing in front of a tidal wave of sinners. He is the one narrow door which we can choose to accept and walk through to a life that is free, with new and different life motives. Making that one choice is the most difficult decision imaginable because somehow we think we are giving up that which is good for something less. In fact, we are handing over the control of our lives, whether good or bad, to God. This action makes us vulnerable in a world where so few have done the same. In accepting God's provision, we accept the pot of gold containing love and direction from God Almighty. We accept the glorious biblical plan from which we were created. Yet immediately we become misunderstood in a world that is threatened by our freedom.

This acceptance expands our vision beyond this temporary life to the forever. The Bible must then become part of us because it is God's Word for us. It is our personal handbook. The Bible is the free living Word for every person in the world. Every individual can read and apply it as if it were written to each alone. Great sermons have been preached on a single verse in the Bible, and the hearers apply its wisdom in millions of ways to their individual lives.

Jesus Christ's birth rules our very calendars. Before His birth the calendar signifies B.C. (Before Christ). A.D. begins around the time of His birth. God is in charge. If you are a believer, take time to renew and revive your original joy of salvation. Cling to the Word of God; read and study it as you've never done before. If you have never accepted Christ as your saving sacrifice, then do it now. This is your day. Stop now and be quiet before the Lord. If you're not sure about all this, ask God in faith to help you to receive Him (Jesus). Tell Him that you want to be assured of salvation and you know that He is your key to entering heaven. Admit to Him that you are a sinner. Believe that He will save you eternally. Confess Christ as Savior and Lord of your life from this day forward.

You are now making a radical decision that will save and deliver you into a new protected way of life beginning immediately. Whether you are rich or poor, you will begin a new focus. Your day-to-day routine will have new meaning. You will understand that whether it is a good or bad day, all days are in God's hands. God will give you wisdom to make right choices that will bring favor to you as you apply the principles of His Word. New ideas for success will come to mind through the prompting of the Holy Spirit. Nothing that happens in your life will be so devastating that God in you will not be able to handle. People might think you're a little crazy with your new thinking, but you can rest assured that God *is* God and He loves you and being His child makes you an heir to His kingdom (Romans 8:17). Your decision not only makes you an heir (owner), but you become adopted into the family of God (Ephesians 1:5). Thank God that He has given you this opportunity and desire. It is a change that will have eternal consequences.

Jesus is the Divider because the world around you will not understand your new attitude. You will be thinking and living on a spiritual level that elevates you to heaven's standard, a standard that is diabolically opposite from the world's. By determining to follow the choice of accepting Jesus, the Christ, as the only acceptable blood sacrifice, your confidence will increase as you read the Bible and receive the teachings of the Holy Spirit. God does not make the Christian life simple. After you accept Christ, you begin the disciplines of a new life of being drawn to God's design through His Word as you gradually drop the worldly baggage and learn a new way of living.

To the Spirit-filled Christian, the truth is so very clear. We are to live our lives in obedience to the Word of God. The world does not want to submit to a higher power. The world gives the false assumption that we can be the master of our own fate. In actuality, the only way to master our own fate is to hand over the control of our lives to the Master of the universe, God. Every godly step is extremely difficult in a noisy world of knowledge which grows in everything except God's Word. The capacity of knowing God is born inside every living human being, but the deadly sin nature abides there as well. God, in His love, allows circumstances to evolve in His human creations to compel them to seek refuge, help, and salvation in their lives. These crises become defining moments. Is this your defining moment?

The world is not offended by the acknowledgment that God exists. However, the battle lines draw at the mention of Jesus Christ. The thought of our having to offer ourselves to and stake our eternity on this once offered pure blood sacrifice repulses an unbelieving world. But if we can somehow muster the wisdom to submit our wills to Christ for eternal salvation, we then realize that even this decision is a gift of love from a holy God. We learn that "We love Him because He first loved us" (1 John 4:19). John 3:16 says it all: "For God so loved the world that He gave His only begotten Son, that whoever believes in Him should not perish but have everlasting life."

Mankind absolutely has no eternal hope unless he accepts the free gift of Jesus Christ. God willingly sacrificed part of Himself for His human creation. Jesus is truly the great Divider, but for those who will receive Him, He is the ticket we need to insure victory in this life and an entrance into the kingdom of God in the hereafter.

The Defeated Foe

When we say, "The devil made me do it," we're almost right, but not quite. The devil is so cunning and masterful in presenting his temptations that we are taken by surprise when we suddenly learn we have been had! When our sin surfaces and is exposed, we try to blame it on everything and everyone else. Adam blamed Eve, Eve blamed the serpent, and we do the same in an effort to excuse ourselves. We, apart from God, are no match for the devil; he wins every time.

Lucifer, the highest of the angels, was created perfect, with great power and brilliance. In eternity before creation, he developed a prideful desire to replace God *(Isaiah 14:12–15)*. He failed to realize that anything created could never take the place of the Creator. Revelation 12 calls Lucifer the great dragon, the serpent, the devil, Satan, and the deceiver. Just as there is a real God, there is a real devil. Satan demeaned God's Word by presenting doubt that resulted in Adam and Eve's disobedience to God, thereby ushering evil into the heart of man. Satan to this day continues his onslaught of evil in his anger and pride against God. That prideful thinking will be his final demise.

God is the God of order. His order was interrupted when mankind received evil, but it did not change His ultimate plan. Just as Adam and Eve were given the freedom to make choices, mankind continues to have the same freedom. As we move forward in this life, it is vitally important that we prepare now and not delay.

That sly old fox, Satan, even uses blessings as a vehicle to curse us. Our lives are filled with modern conveniences and entertainment. A moment of total quietness seldom exists in our lives. When we move from one place to another, we avoid the quietness by turning on the radio or television; or we busy ourselves with projects, shopping, talking, etc. Quietness becomes an enemy. This kind of loudness is hollow and empty like a drum. Noise masks the inevitable ticking of the clock that is slowly racing toward the end of this life.

Most people live as though they are on a merry-go-round. They go up and down, round and round, to the same music. Children are taught that to be happy and successful, they must get the best education to get the best job in order to buy the best stuff and retire at an early age. This is fantasy. True wealth is achieved only when there is inner peace. Inner peace resides in those who have chosen God's plan and who practice that plan. There are no shortcuts.

If this is disturbing to you, now is the time to choose. Satan would have you to discount this reading as a myth or something far-out. He will actually put the thought in your mind not to believe any of this. Whether or not you want to believe it does not change the truth that God *is* God and His plan is unfolding daily. The plan is not a secret either. It is spelled out in the Bible. Now is the time; consider yourself special that you have the opportunity to jump off the merry-go-round into a life that will grant you happiness and contentment here and now and assurance of royalty in the kingdom of God. It is not a half-hearted commitment but one that removes you from the throne of your life to a total surrender to Jehovah God through the blood of Jesus Christ.

When you make that decision, you will become a new person (2 Corinthians 5:17). To begin growing in your new life, the Bible will be God's personal Word to you. It will become alive in a way that you will think it was written to you alone. When you read about things in the Bible that sound unbelievable, just know that the problem is not in the Bible itself, but it is in your current understanding of it. The Bible is the living Word. The principles of the Bible are truth, and they bring life to the believer. The Bible has been researched, studied, and read more than any other book in the world. Prophesies written hundreds of years before their actual occurrences have come to pass exactly as foretold every time.

As you begin your new life, you change from the inside out. You are new inside, but your day-to-day routine will remain the same. You will get up daily, go to school or work as you have before, but you will have a different outlook. This early beginning is a critical time because when you leave the kingdom of darkness, the devil wakes up. He will try to use others to put you down, rob your joy, and oppress you. When you experience such attacks (and you will), simply tell him that he is finished with you. You have received the living Lord Jesus Christ, and there will be no turning back to a life that goes nowhere but to hell. When doubts attack, you are assured victory when you open your Bible and read verses such as Revelation 20:10, God's promise to the devil, that old fox, that he will be cast into the lake of fire and brimstone to be tormented day and night forever and ever. He cannot handle that! He'll flee from you! Even in his pride and deceitful wickedness, Satan knows only too well the truth of his future.

You must develop a talking relationship with God. When you feel a tendency to fall back into your former lifestyle, ask God for His strength to keep you on track. With practice, you will learn to love the Lord, His people, the church, and life in a way that you have never experienced.

The devil will try to put you down with thoughts of guilt, unworthiness, sinfulness, etc. When these thoughts drift into your mind, simply search the scriptures for help regarding the subject at hand. Anything that puts a negative heavy weight on your heart is not of God. That weight is an attempt of Satan to drag you back to your old life. You can learn fast to defeat the old foe. His only place is under your feet. You have a new Hero in your life.

Satan is allowed until the end of the age to accuse us before the throne of God (Revelation 12) and to roam the earth (1 Peter 5:8), seeking whom he may devour. However, our very choice to accept and believe God through His one perfect sacrifice, Jesus Christ, protects us in righteousness. Satan's influence on our lives is dependent on our choice to accept or reject that one sacrifice. Thank God for the freedom of choice because it shows God's confidence in us to choose His way, and choosing His way will assure our victory in this life and the blessings of heaven.

Satan and his demons can possess the unbeliever, but he can only oppress the believer. You see, on this earth there are two kingdoms from which to choose. Since we are born with a sin nature, it is easier to choose Satan's way because it requires no discipline. It comes naturally. However, God builds within us a void that can be filled only by His Spirit. It is God's intention that we develop and use our God-given intelligence to His glory. If we do, then we will have fulfilled our life's purpose.

Although babies are born with a sin nature, they are blameless before God because of their innocence. It is God's design that parents rear their children in reverence to Him. God gave mankind dominion over all living things (Genesis 1:28), including the nurturing of babies. God does not change or alter His Word. Sometimes we think He does, but that is a misnomer. Once He speaks, it is eternal. If babies are cared for physically and mentally and are brought up to accept the way of the Lord, when they develop to the age we call the age of accountability, they are naturally inclined to continue in the way they have been taught. If not, they will follow their sinful inclinations. It is unnecessary to teach children to do wrong; doing wrong is innate and natural. Since mankind has a sinful nature, we must be taught to do right.

At a certain time in all people's lives, God gives them the opportunity to accept Him and be forgiven for their sins. God is always the pursuer. We do not have the capacity to pursue Him. We love Him because He first loved us (1 John 4:19). Hebrews 11:6 states that "without faith it is impossible to please Him, for he who comes to God must believe that He is, and that He is a rewarder of those who diligently seek Him." Believing is more than mental assent. When we truly believe in something, it becomes part of us.

Satan is a liar and a deceiver. If he cannot get you to outright refuse to accept the Lord, then he will try to entice you to put off the decision. This is your opportunity to see Satan for who he is. He spreads his pride like seeds in an open field. He fools people by the millions into thinking they are the masters of their lives. Look at the deception of that concept. Do you have control of your next breath or heartbeat?

The devil might be trying to remind you of people you have known who have professed to be Christians and who have turned out to be the worst sinners who ever lived. Yes, there are all kinds of failures. Some people wear the badge of Christianity but have no idea who Christ is. Some are born again (receiving Christ in their hearts) but have fallen by cleverly designed schemes of Satan. When this happens, the hearts of onlookers feel much confusion. God is the righteous Judge, however; and He will in due time deal with the sins of the just and the unjust.

2 Corinthians 5:17 says, "if anyone is in Christ, he is a new creation; old things have passed away; behold, all things have become new." At that decision point, the person is saved eternally because that most important required life decision has been made.

Although Satan is alive and well, he is a defeated foe. It is only a matter of time until he will be cast into hell with his angels and followers (Revelation 20:10). Unbelievers who refuse to accept Christ become hard of heart and go out into eternity damned by the ploy of Satan. Hell was designed for only Satan and his angels. It was not created for anyone else. People choose to go to hell by rejecting God's provision for salvation. Christ in God reigns supreme, and those who are smart enough to accept Him will enjoy everything the Bible reveals about the kingdom of God.

Satan is the angel of the dark. He is on the minus side of life. He brings death. To prove the point, list on a paper every dark, negative, and sinful thing which you can think. Title the list "Satan Attributes." Begin this list with the word "Hell." Include on the list subtle things such as apathy, doubt, insecurity, fear, etc. Make another list entitled "God Attributes." On this list, begin with the word "Heaven." List positive attributes such as love, light, sun, good, riches, building, strength, etc. Meditate on the two lists. Who, in his right mind, would pursue anything other than the positive list?

Satan achieves his purpose in the negative. He will use any tactic to achieve that purpose. Although he uses the "do nothing" tactic as his most successful tool, he is not above tempting people to do good things for the wrong reasons. One example would be "work." Work is honorable, but to work merely to get the next dollar to either hoard or consume on ourselves would be defeating because that void would be impossible to fill. Satan's way can never satisfy enough, achieve enough, or do enough. He brings hopelessness, sadness, and, finally, the abyss.

God instructs us in Romans 12:9 to "Abhor what is evil. Cling to what is good." God is a passionate God who gives us every opportunity to choose life. 2 Thessalonians 3:3 says, "the Lord is faithful, who will establish you and guard you from the evil one."

Restful Fight

Opposition, contention, unrest, and war are bound in the hearts of men. The enormity of world problems is escalating to the point that we often feel helpless about contributing anything to making situations better. In the midst of the unrest, the law of the land rules, and we are subject to it. God established the law in His infinite wisdom because of sin and gave mankind authority on the earth under the law, but He reminds us in Psalm 24:1 that "The earth is the Lord's, and all its fullness: the world and those that dwell therein." Psalm 66:7 explains that "He rules by His power forever; His eyes observe the nations." Also, in Psalm 103:19, the Lord tells us that He "has established His throne in heaven, and His kingdom rules over all." Though God has given the nations freedom to carry out His law, when they rebel, He will let them go only so far before He intervenes. This intervention is for their good and preservation.

If nations would understand and submit to the order which God set out in the writings of Scripture, peace would prevail. But mankind, in his sinful nature, breaks the law. All lawbreakers actually rebel against God since He is the Maker of the law. Courts of law are given authority to decide justice. Is every court decision right and just? The answer would be "no" because humans are in charge of the judgments and the best of them are clouded by sin. Yet, God allows

His human creation to rule the earth, and we individuals are free from the penalty of the law when we abide by it.

We might not rule a nation, but we are responsible for decisions and actions in our personal lives. Every nation is strengthened when its citizens make and live by right choices. Sometimes decisions create adverse results. This happens in all of our lives at one time or another. Grace and mercy must be the motto over the Spirit-filled believer.

When mistakes or disagreements occur, the believer is to quickly reconcile in obedience to the Bible. If God can forgive from a lifetime of sin those who receive His Son, then we certainly should forgive others, whatever the occurrence. All redeemed sinners have been given forgiveness and salvation by a holy God who simply forgets our sins and accepts us as sinless. Ephesians 4:26–27 gives seldom taken but winning advice to the reader: "Be angry, and do not sin: do not let the sun go down on your wrath, nor give place to the devil."

Forgiveness brings peace to the spirit, soul, and body. No offence is worthy of sleepless nights of hashing and rehashing an offence. Unsettled differences kill the spirit and make the body sick. Today, begin a practice of extending prompt forgiveness when you are offended. In the end, you will be freer and healthier than most other people in your world. Matthew 5:9 says, "Blessed are the peacemakers, for they shall be called sons of God."

World standards are polar opposites of true Christ standards. Although the world looks at the symbol of the church with respect, it has little appreciation of the strength of the real believers in Christ who sit in its pews. When we launch out in faith to a new life in Christ, inner peace, new motives, and understanding are born in us. That newness is created because the Comforter, called the Holy Spirit, comes into our lives. One would think that life would be easy from that point. We do bask on a bed of roses, but thorns are on that bed as well.

Much is written in the Bible about enemies. Does the family of God have enemies? Oh, yes! And our greatest enemy is the devil. He will use any tactic available to hinder God's plan. God has allowed Satan this period of time as a vehicle to actually confirm His own eternal victory.

In eternity past Satan was created top archangel in heaven, and he is brilliant. We are no match for him apart from the power of the Holy Spirit, the third part of God that resides in us. The Holy Spirit forever abides in every believer. We rest in the assurance that when the devil himself or anyone he uses comes against us, the battle is the Lord's (1 Samuel 17:47). We can actually rest in the fact that no one can hurt us when God's power is in us.

This world is in a constant battle between good and evil because the devil is "the prince of the power of the air" (Ephesians 2:2). The Bible provides great detail about fighting and dealing with the enemy. Military terms throughout the pages of scripture describe people at war. God instructs His people to "Put on the whole armor of God, that you may be able to stand against the wiles of the devil. For we do not wrestle against flesh and blood, but against principalities, against powers, against the rulers of the darkness of this age, against spiritual hosts of wickedness in the heavenly places" (Ephesians 6:11–12).

The believer's method of fighting is quite different from the world's way. The believer's armor for battle is faith, truth, and righteousness: knowing the gospel, being saved, and applying the Word of God. By being dressed in this unusual armor, we have the power to stand victorious in evil days (Ephesians 6:13–16).

Believers are to "Fight the good fight of faith" through righteousness (being right with God), godliness (resembling God's character), faith (believing God), love (loving as He loves), patience (having no forceful intentions), and gentleness (remaining clear-headed under mental fire) that we may lay hold of eternal life (1 Timothy 6:11–12).

When soldiers join the military, they immediately begin all training necessary (in body and spirit) to defend and protect their country—to the point of death, if necessary. Allegiance to country becomes their life. They surrender on duty personal rights to a greater cause. God's military is composed of His angels who continually serve at His command. Believers are not in heaven's military, as they are God's sons and daughters who are called to be heirs, kings, and priests who will rule and reign with Him in eternity (Revelation 5:10 and Revelation 22:5). In the military, soldiers can appeal only to their immediate officer, whereas in God's army, the angels are in constant communication with the Commander and Chief, who is Christ. Until the end of the age in which we live, our one and only responsibility is to surrender our lives in obedience to the King of kings and Lord of lords who fights for us. Our handbook of strategies is the Bible. God keeps no secrets from His family. The Bible reveals it all; but only the believer can understand, as the Holy Spirit is the teacher and He dwells only in the children of God. His ear is always open to our prayers, and He is eager to answer.

God is the God of the past, present, and future. When we join the trinity—Father, Son, and Holy Spirit (the three in One)—we begin a new life with Him that begins at the point of our accepting Him; and the new life never ends. We become heaven-bound eternal beings, and this life is simply our beginning. Life on earth is boot camp for eternity, but it is what we do with what we know that determines our placement in the world to come (Matthew 25:21).

It is God's intention that we live our lives in total dependence on Him. The burden is His. We can rest as we wait for His return for us. Christ compels us in Matthew 11:28–30 to "Come unto Me, all you who labor and are heavy laden, and I will give you rest. Take My yoke upon you and learn from Me; for I am gentle and lowly in heart, and you will find rest for your souls. For My yoke is easy, and My burden is light."

Believers are to strive only in their efforts to obey God's Word. In doing so, they will one day enter into heaven's rest. They can then quote 2 Timothy 4:7–8 as the apostle Paul wrote, "I have fought a good fight, I have finished the race, I have kept the faith. Finally, there is laid up for me the crown of righteousness, which the Lord, the righteous Judge, will give to me on that Day, and not to me only but also to all who have loved His appearing."

Surviving the Church

The symbol of Christianity is the cross. It stands at the pinnacle of every Christ-honoring church steeple. The cross represents the complete sacrifice of Jesus Christ for all mankind. Church doors open wide to receive all who choose to enter. The very appearance of church buildings brings a peace and rest that few other structures provide. It is the house of God.

Hebrews 10:25 instructs us not to forsake the assembling of ourselves together. The church is the place where we assemble. Exodus 20:8, the Fourth Commandment, states, "Remember the Sabbath day, to keep it holy." Verse 10 says that it "is the Sabbath of the Lord your God. In it you shall do no work," and verse 11 compares God resting on the seventh day of creation to the importance of mankind having a day of rest. Most churchgoers would agree that life is better when they honor the Lord by attending church and stepping away from their normal work routine one day a week. By honoring that one commandment, we are energized to do a better job for the next six days.

Churches come in all shapes, sizes, and styles of worship. Although the methods of worship may vary, the teaching must be true to Scripture. Corporately joining others in hearing and responding to the Word of God encourages worshipers and strengthens their spirit. Corporate worship actually becomes a school with its textbook being the Bible. It teaches not only history and intellectual truths but principles that lead to solutions to the issues of life.

Although the church is the very place where people go for the purpose of worshiping God, all are not there for that reason. Since the devil is the accuser of the brethren before the throne in heaven (Revelation 12:10), wouldn't it be his business to attend church as well? Yet, rest assured the devil's work will never survive on God's turf. The church belongs to God, and He will insure its overall protection. The believer's command is simply to go and leave the rest to the Lord.

Every church is a unique living body with a definite personality. God unites the various members of churches in one spirit for His glory and purpose. When the Lord leads new members to a certain church, they will enjoy contentment as they are a godly fit in personality and spirit. They immediately feel at home in the fellowship as they contribute to the work of God by using their gifts and talents for the good of His church.

When pastors, elders, priests, etc., begin work in a new church, the church body readily embraces and accepts them; but the spirit of the leadership must quickly merge in concert to the likeness of the church body. If a new church leader fails to be sensitive to the church's personality, chaos and unrest set in like a slow cancer. This insensitivity brings judgment from the leaders that the church is uncaring or uncooperative with their leading, while all along, it is simply a difference of personality.

The church is referred to by such names as the children of God, the family of God, the flock, the body and bride of Christ, etc. By inference, God's design is that we live and work together in love in order to grow the church. All born-again church members enter their new life with bondage that must be peeled away one layer at a time until they become free in Christ. It is true that when we give our lives to Christ, we are totally forgiven; but just as a child begins the process of learning at birth, the newborn believer must do the same.

41

Many new believers enter the church with high expectations. The fire that burns within them is radical. The Word is alive in them as nothing else has been before. They expect the church to be on fire as well, only to discover, in their own eyes, a lesser fire. This zeal and energy in their newfound lives must grow and develop as the Holy Spirit leads them into His purpose. The fire that burns within the heart is set by God Himself, and it is the challenge and responsibility of everyone in the church body to fuel that flame in honor of the King of kings and Lord of lords.

Church leaders have a grave responsibility in leading the church. Their calling requires that they be the continual example of Christlikeness. They are called to be transparent in their ministry as they lead scripturally. Every sermon they preach is a sermon that first should flood their own hearts.

In the church body, some members are more spiritually mature than others. However, true leaders are called to the privilege of scripturally growing the entire body no matter their level of maturity. All members whom God brings into the church are unique, having varying degrees of maturity. The church must be equipped to teach and lead every believer without partiality in order that the body grows to completeness in the plan of God and to His glory.

Today the world system greatly influences the church. The world looks attractive and harmless, but the dangers lie just beneath its surface. Christ Himself informs us in Mark 7:21–23 that "out of the heart of men proceed evil thoughts, adulteries, fornications, murders, thefts, covetousness, wickedness, deceit, lewdness, an evil eye, blasphemy, pride, foolishness. All these evil things come from within and defile a man." Every action is birthed from a thought. The challenge to the church is to root out evil through the power of the Word.

Many church leaders are bound by prideful strongholds that affect their entire ministry. These strongholds are issues of unresolved reconciliations, bitterness, secret sins, etc. The root of these is pride.

Proverbs 16:18 says, "Pride goes before destruction, and a haughty spirit before a fall." God blesses the church that is led by a transparent leadership who is right with Him. Christ gives a refreshing promise in Matthew 5:8: "Blessed are the pure in heart, for they shall see God." When the leadership leads God's way, the people will follow.

The single focus on God is the main issue for believers when they join and become members of a church congregation. Though we long to put our trust and confidence in fellow believers, including church leadership, we soon learn that it must be in God alone. People are fallible, and our failings become quite obvious as we become active in the church body.

Although many in the congregation are born again and desire to live their lives pleasing to God, the cares and circumstances of life bring pressures that divert their attention to simple humanistic survival techniques. Rather than turning to the source of power, the Bible, for answers, they become confused and defeated. This is when the church should become a spiritual hospital where the sin sickness can be treated, but cure only comes when the right medicines are used. These medicines are found in applying the principles of Scripture.

Being an active part of a church congregation over a lifetime is difficult, but it is God's plan. Romans 12:2 says, "do not be conformed to this world; but be transformed by the renewing of your mind, that you may prove what is that good and acceptable and perfect will of God." Just as the physical body needs to be fed daily, so does the mind. The pure truth from the Bible must be ingested daily in order to maintain spiritual health and balance. As we become biblically strong, we receive wisdom to see through problems that we could not have solved had we not turned to the source of all wisdom and strength. If we are spiritually equipped, we will remain so when the winds of controversy invade the church body.

Since the crucifixion and resurrection of Christ, we have been living in the last days.

2 Timothy 3 warns that in the final days there will be trouble and stress. People will be lovers of self and self-centered, lovers of money and aroused by an inordinate desire for wealth, proud and arrogant, etc. The Spirit-filled believer desires God's will above his own. The lost person is plagued with spiritual blindness. Christians come across as weaklings to him, but God calls them pillars of strength. Meekness is not weakness; it is the height of strength. When one stops a disagreement without having to say the last word, that is meekness personified.

Sometimes scriptural error is allowed and even preached in the house of God. When we find ourselves in that kind of situation, it is time to search for a church that is scripturally sound. It is imperative, however, that we are led by Scripture to know the will of God. Before changing churches, believers need to give prayerful attention to the decision in order to avoid making a wrong judgment.

Early in the spiritual growth process, we come to realize that the responsibility for the strength of the church lies in each individual's growing relationship with God through Christ. No two people are alike. All have differing talents and gifts to be used to the glory of God. What better place to use them than in the church?

Healthy spiritual growth brings us to the knowledge that the Lord seeks us; we do not seek Him because it is not our nature. Every person who reaches the age of accountability receives the opportunity to accept or reject Christ. Whether we accept Him on a church pew or in the darkest corner of our lives, we accept the responsibility of living the Christ life. A growing believer will attend and serve in the church in obedience to God's Word.

When difficulties arise in the church, unless it is a doctrinal error, we are to stand firm, pray, and wait on the Lord. The easy thing to do would be to leave for a different church or to quit altogether. As long as we live on earth, all churches will undergo problems because sinful people make up the corporate church. In God's economy, there is but one church; and it is made up of people who accept His Son and believe His Word. God's true church is made up of believers who are spread out all over the world. Problems are resolved as we give them over to the Lord. It is His church, and He will take care of it. We are to continue in our faithfulness to the Lord in the difficult times. In doing so, we grow to become spiritual pillars of the church who produce the fruit of the Spirit (Galatians 5:23–24). We can then look back on problems as giant steps to spiritual wisdom. The church needs pillars of wisdom to make it strong.

The short book of James in the New Testament is packed with instructions to the believer. In chapter 3, it instructs us not to be teachers over more than we are spiritually able to handle because we are held to a stricter accountability. Leaders in the church are highly respected and sometimes idolized by sincere onlookers. If the leaders are not careful, they become proud in their status; and Satan easily sets them up for a disgraceful fall, thereby causing much shame and disgrace. Amid the ups and downs, however, it is the responsibility of every believer to remain faithful to God as he survives the church.

Patient Persistence

Every great success story began with a dream. Children easily express their life dreams with a sense of innocence and freedom that brings an unconscious hope to the hearts of the hearers. However, hindrances to those dreams invade them slowly as society pours these children into its mold. Social environment influences us to the extent that we are not only surrounded by it, but it becomes the actual substance that seemingly sustains us. Every living human being is blessed with dreams that, if pursued to the fullest, would bring fulfillment that would be heaven on earth to them. Pursuing a dream is very difficult because from the beginning our strengths and weaknesses are tested as the dream develops into reality. Pursuit takes sacrificial effort, discipline, and tenacity. If we succeed, it is a miracle.

The dreams we are talking about are those desires born deep in our hearts. These dreams are wrapped-up talents, gifts, and abilities that we receive from the living God above. Many have grasped and pursued their dreams to the end that they have achieved monetary or intellectual success but have been left empty because they have never realized or known that there is more to their dreams. It is only when the dreamer discovers the source and purpose of the dream that he can enjoy total success.

True success is true wealth; but it is not measured in this world's dollars and cents, although it could be part of it. Proverbs 23:4 tells us not to labor to be rich and to cease from our own wisdom. One who pursues a dream must look to the Maker of dreams for divine wisdom and knowledge. If our goal is that of only making money, it spells ultimate failure. The goal must be to produce that which will benefit others and glorify the God of that goal. When this combination is achieved, it becomes true success.

True wealth is built by patient persistence, just as a contractor would build a strong house. It doesn't just happen, and it doesn't happen overnight. From the initial house dream, plans are drawn, and step by step the work continues until the final walk-through. If nothing happens beyond the dream, however, the house will never be built.

Proverbs 13:4 says it this way, the "soul of a lazy man desires, and has nothing; but the soul of the diligent shall be made rich." There is no room in the building of wealth for the lazy. Proverbs 13:11 goes on to state that "he who gathers by labor will increase."

For a dream to be born, much attention, energy, and time must be given to it. From the initial vision to the final goal, the course must be pursued with single focus. Working persistently toward the success of the dream is exhaustive; and many fall by the wayside from fear of failing, generalizing and losing focus, or allowing lesser things to invade and smother its reality.

In a culture where "we want it and we want it now" prevails, patience is foreign. But in order to achieve our intended goal, patience is a most important ingredient in the mix of success. Every day, the one who pursues a dream must look up and know that his dream is a gift from God. Yet, just as God provides food for birds, He simply does not drop it into their mouths. They must search for it. In the same way, as we live our lives, we must search with patience and diligence for ways that would move us toward the realization of our life's purpose and dreams.

The entire book of Proverbs consists of wisdom keys. Wisdom is the ability to live life skillfully. Proverbs is a Bible book that every entrepreneur should read over and over again as his dream breaks into reality. God is the giver of all wisdom, and we are foolish to think that we can attain it from any other source. We might gain worldly knowledge, but true wisdom comes from God.

In the Bible's power-packed little book of James, we read in chapter 1 that the "testing of your faith produces patience. But let patience have its perfect work, that you may be perfect and complete, lacking nothing." Would that be heaven on earth to have neither external nor internal need? Then in James 1:5 we read, "If any of you lacks wisdom, let him ask of God, who gives to all liberally and without reproach, and it will be given to him." This requires much focus and determination on the part of the one asking, but verse 6 says, "let him ask in faith, with no doubting, for he who doubts is like a wave of the sea driven and tossed by the wind. For let not that man suppose that he will receive anything from the Lord."

As we actively pursue our life purpose (dream), we should view and manage everything else in daily living not with the speed of the hare or the slowness of the tortoise but with the patient persistence of time itself. Time is in no hurry as it moves along with awesome consistency. It cannot be rushed, nor can it be slowed. Time is given to us in twenty-four-hour cycles, and it is given to everyone equally. Opportunity is encompassed within these cycles of time, but more often than not we pass it by without the slightest glance.

When we look back at the time we already have been given and at how much of it we have wasted, we cannot help becoming depressed. Think about it! Seconds, minutes, hours, days, weeks, months, years, and even decades have passed us by with our having utilized only a fraction of it. Yet, the Bible gives solace in showing us that the next moment of our lives is a new opportunity to become. We see this in verses such as Psalm 40:1–3: "I waited patiently for the Lord; and He inclined to me, and heard my cry. He also brought me up out of a horrible pit, out of the miry clay, and set my feet upon a rock, and established my steps. He has put a new song in my mouth—praise to our God; many will see it and fear, and will trust in the Lord."

The earthly age of mankind means nothing to God. He is time-less. Pursuing God's purpose is one that has no age limitation. From the youngest to the oldest, the next moment is a free gift; and it is one to be pursued with a God-given goal in mind.

This is your golden opportunity to join God in maximizing your spot on His great timetable. Look at the grand scheme of things. 2 Corinthians 5:17–18 says, "if any man is in Christ, he is a *new* creation; old things have passed away; behold, all things have become new. Now all things are of God, who has reconciled us to Himself through Jesus Christ..." We, *new* creatures, can start afresh and anew, "forgetting those things which are behind and reaching forward to those things which are ahead, I press toward the goal for the prize of the upward call of God in Christ Jesus. Therefore let us, as many as are mature, have this mind; and if in anything you think otherwise, God will reveal even this to you" (Philippians 3:13–15).

Yes, God gives us our dreams; and if we ever truly live them out, it will be through a full reliance on the Word of God. The wealth of life is attained when we actively, patiently, and persistently seek the plan of God for our lives. The only way to do this is to methodically read the Bible as the absolute truth written to you personally. It will lead you into free, victorious living for the rest of your life, on this side of eternity and on the other side as well.

Your invitation to step onto God's timetable is immediate. It is not by force, but only a fool would allow it to pass by. If you accept this invitation, secure a notebook and turn to its last page. Write the following three questions and answer each in detail:

Where am I?

Where do I want to go?

How will I get there?

Turn to the front of the notebook and date the first page. Begin journaling daily your success course. Review the last page daily as well to help you keep focus. Alongside your notebook will be the Bible. After giving your life to Christ for His salvation and lordship, you will be ready to begin real living—living that will bring fulfillment and even a ticklish joy as you pursue His will. You will realize that your personal sins of the past, present, and future are all willfully forgotten by God as you learn to trust His Word. With a clean slate, all past remembrances can become stepping stones in your victorious pursuit. You can indeed have it all! Everything actually has been done for you—you are simply to walk it out with your Maker.

Health

8-19-19 Praying for Gloria (the author of this book) who today is in the hospital. She has been battling cancer for some time.

When you have your health, you have everything! How many times have you heard that? It is true that good health is vital to our well-being, and we give much attention to it. Think about how much you yourself have spent in the area of health—for example, doctor and hospital bills, insurance, prescriptions, over-the-counter drug purchases, health club memberships, sports clothing, exercise equipment, diet books, health books, magazines, etc. Yes, and now we can purchase everything from A to Z over the internet. Health care is big business, and we spend a large portion of our annual income on it. Ask yourself this question, "How much of what I've spent have I benefited from?"

In the last century we have had a knowledge explosion unparalleled in the history of mankind. We have every resource imaginable, but the fact is we are still sick. The irony is that we still can't cure the common cold! So obviously, the answer to health and healing cannot be left to mankind's devices alone. Here again we are drawn to a higher source, the Giver of life, for answers.

In Matthew 7:7, Jesus is not at all speaking in the area of health, but here we can learn principles that will lead us to solving medical matters. He says, "Ask, and it will be given to you; seek, and you will find; knock, and it will be opened to you." He assures us in verse 8 of

Matthew 7 that "everyone who asks receives and he who seeks finds and to him who knocks it will be opened." The issues of life may overtake us, but every one of them can be solved when we apply the truths of the Word. Radical as it is in our day and time, the genuine prescription for every need in our lives is found in the Bible.

Answers to our questions do not come casually, but Jeremiah 29:13 says, "you will seek Me *(God)* and find Me, when you search for Me with all your heart." Breaking into this higher relationship with the King of kings is available to all, but only a few will submit to what it takes to receive the full benefit of attaining God's blessings, including the coveted health blessing.

We want to be healthy but do little more than attain head knowledge about our physical well-being. We drift along, failing to address the very elemental rules of health and wellness, and are shocked and surprised when our bodies break down because of abuse. Although obesity is rampant in the United States, it is just one of the results of abusing our health. Many of those who are pencil thin are subject to high blood pressure, cholesterol, and sugar, bulimia, anorexia, etc. Other health problems occur as a result of smoking, drinking, and other drug abuses. It is amazing that the body is as resilient as it is.

For the majority of people, getting on the right track to good health is directly related to diet. The scriptures address this matter. In Deuteronomy, chapter 14, God gave the children of Israel dietary instructions as they were on their way to the promised land. Today, the world can benefit from these important principles of truth. In verse 2, God told the Jewish people that they were chosen people, set apart for Himself. In the New Testament, Romans 11 refers to Israel as an olive tree. Through their unbelief, some of them were cut off; and the Gentiles were grafted in. Any non-Jew is a Gentile. So by inference, the principles of the entire Word were written for the Jew and Gentile, inclusively, because of this grafting in.

Deuteronomy 14

The Food and Drug Administration (FDA) is strict on proper packaging and preserving of food. However, the more we do to help ourselves in this area, the more questions seem to arise. Residue from plastic is under continual study, while dyes and chemicals used to increase the shelf life of foods have proven to work adversely as many people are allergic to these dyes and chemicals. How did the world survive before the FDA? Could it be that in the generations before they asked God's blessing over the food before eating it? According to the American Heritage Dictionary, to bless means "to make holy by religious rite, sanctify." One of the meanings for blessing is "to preserve from evil," and this is exactly what we are asking God to do each time we say grace.

As we look in scripture, nearly every book includes words of blessing to the believer. If we truly have a heart of blessing toward others, we generate transparency and purity which lead to healthy relationships. When we ask God for a blessing, how much more is the blessing! In protecting ourselves in the area of the food we eat, much illness would be avoided if we would simply bow our heads and say grace (make holy or cleanse) over every bite of food we eat.

With the elimination of the "blessing" at mealtimes, sickness and disease have escalated. But what would people think if you began this daily practice? It might open up an opportunity to teach others how to protect themselves against being affected by the impurities in food. This is radical, but it is worth gold as far as your health is concerned. We must, just as Joshua issued the decision challenge to the children of Israel in Joshua 24:15, "Choose for yourselves this day whom you will serve… But as for me and my house, we will serve the Lord."

In Deuteronomy 14:3 God instructs people not to eat anything that is abominable to the Lord. Abomination is a strong word, meaning that which is detestable or loathsome. He doesn't just make a general statement; He lists specifics. Among today's popular meats that are listed on Deuteronomy's "do not eat" list are pork and shellfish.

Many view the Old Testament as not applicable in this generation, as we are living in a different age, the Age of Grace or the Church Age. However, the Old Testament is part of the complete truth; and once God makes a statement, the depth of its meaning reaches to all generations.

After Moses relayed to the children of Israel God's dietary laws in Deuteronomy 14, disobedience to them was a sin against God. But under the new covenant set forth by Jesus in the New Testament, it was no longer a sin to eat any and all meats. So where is the deeper meaning for not eating such things as pork and shellfish? Pork and high blood pressure sing to the same tune, as do shellfish and cholesterol. With the abundance of food in our grasp, would it be too much of a sacrifice to pass up these two items in the interest of health? Deuteronomy 14 lists all good and bad meats. Because they have never read this part of the Bible, many people do not realize these lists exist; but on investigation, they will quickly see that we do eat and like most of the good meats listed and we do not eat those that are listed as bad meats. It would seem wise to observe all of Deuteronomy 14 for the blessing of health.

Perhaps the healthiest food diet has never been published. It is a "no combinations" diet. On this diet, one would be free to eat reasonable servings of all allowable meats of Deuteronomy 14 and all vegetables, fruits, and nuts, simply seasoned with butter, salt, pepper, and herbs. Whole-grain bread would be the only combination allowable because throughout Scripture, bread is a blessed food. This diet would give maximum nutrition without high fat and calories.

Salads are combinations. What would be wrong with eating a tossed salad? In order to satisfy our palates, we must douse them with good-tasting dressings, and that "combination" simply defeats the purpose. Casseroles are delicious and slide down easily; but when we think about the fat content, we simply close our minds, hope for the best, and eat them anyway. Desserts come in all kinds of combinations, filled with health threats on every side! Beverages come in many combinations as well. Heaven provides radical freeing truth regarding "no combinations."

There are those who believe that God is not involved in the details of our lives and that we are victims of circumstance. Psalm 139:15 intimately states, "My frame was not hidden from You, when I was made in secret, and skillfully wrought in the lowest parts of the earth." God was present at our very conception! James 4:8 instructs us to "Draw near to God, and He will draw near to you." God is the God of details. He sees everything and desires the best in His awesome love for us, but we have the privilege of either accepting or rejecting His leadership in our lives.

Health and healing are very important; and when we are sick, we realize just how helpless we are. The most important healing is that which Christ paid on our behalf. He came to earth knowing the life that lay ahead as Isaiah had prophesied years before. Isaiah 53:5 states that "by His stripes we are healed." Years later, 1 Peter 2:24 confirms Isaiah's prophesy by stating "by Whose stripes you were healed." Everything in our lives is microscopically known by God. Our healing is in the Lord.

A healthy spirit is one that depends on the Word of God for life itself. Just as physical food is necessary for the body, spiritual food is necessary for the spirit. Many of the physical ailments in our lives would be healed if stress and anxiety in the spirit were treated with scripture.

Proverbs 3:7–8 says, "Do not be wise in your own eyes; fear [reverence] the Lord, and depart from evil. It will be health to your flesh, and strength to your bones."

Proverbs 16:24 is equally strong: "Pleasant words are like a honeycomb, sweetness to the soul and health to the bones." If we trust the Lord and do what is right with a pleasing attitude, we receive health and healing. Proverbs 12:18 says, "…the tongue of the wise promotes health." True wisdom comes only from God.

If you have good health, do all to maintain it; and if you are in need of it, do all to gain it. The mystery to achieving a healthy mind and body is in the Word of God. There are no shortcuts. Start today.

May God's Words
Do all to gain good health

Deut. 31:6 Be strong and courageou
Do not be afraid or terrified
because of Them, for The Lord
God goes with you; He will
never leave you.

2 Thess. 3:16
Now may The Lord of peace
himself give you peace at
all times and in every way.
The Lord be with all of you.

Wealth

In this microwave age of instant gratification, it will be radical to change gears and join God in His absolute, perfect plan for your life. Millions have tried it their way, pounding out their existence as if it were all up to them, only to come to the end of life perplexed that there was nothing more to it. Every person was born with a purpose. There has never been an accidental birth. Once there is conception, another puzzle piece of life is added to God's grand picture and plan.

Trusting God is essential as we refocus and begin living Matthew 6:33 to "seek first the kingdom of God, and His righteousness, and all these things shall be added to you." Can you believe that there is a way that is not your own? Would it be liberating to shift the responsibility of life over to the Ancient of days, who is well equipped to bless you with His success plan for your life? 3 John 2 says, "Beloved, I pray that you may prosper in all things and be in health, just as your soul prospers." In order to see His plan for us, we must release control and trust the Lord.

Statistics prove that most people do not like their vocations. They would rather be doing something else. Bondage wraps around us one layer at a time until we are seemingly helpless to seek change. Young people acquire a job based on how much money they can make with the educational skills they have. They begin acquiring "things" that require more things; and they become overextended in their credit, which binds them to a job that is not one they find remotely fulfilling. To further complicate the matter, a serious relationship develops into marriage. The idea of two salaries being better than one is attractive, but the truth arrives too late. More debt ensues with each acquisition, and each acquisition requires more things to be thrown out. Many spend the rest of their lives enslaved to their jobs and in every kind of bondage while wishing things were different.

If you are catching the wisdom of any of this, today is the day to evaluate your life. Simply determine to begin seeking and finding the life that was mapped out for you before the beginning of time. God wants you to prosper, but true prosperity is accomplished God's way. It cannot be brought about by cunning devices you drum up on your own. Handing over to God the authority in your life means that you acknowledge that your way is not the best way. This surrender to God means you will unload all the baggage you are carrying—some good and some bad.

Christ is the Word, and the Word is the truth, and the truth is the Bible, the true living Word of God. Christ says in John 14:6, "I am the way, the truth, and the life. No one comes to the Father except through Me." So it is His way or no way.

Evaluate your personal life. Refer again to your notebook with the questions:

Where am I?

Where do I want to go?

How will I get there?

List and consider everything—finances, health, and relationships.

List your heartfelt dreams for the future. Your dreams will become positives for some of the negatives that you wrote under "Where am I?" Be specific.

When you get to "How will I get there?" top this list with *Search the Scriptures.* Then continue by listing every way you can think of to attain your dream.

As you begin, you must address certain issues. If you are living a sinful lifestyle that you know is wrong, you need to deal with it. Do the right thing in honor of God. If you sincerely do that, He will honor you in the other tough areas. 2 Peter 2:9 says, "the Lord knows how to deliver the godly out of temptations." The goal is to walk a straight line amid the highs and lows of life's circumstances. This can be done only as you walk with Christ.

Your life is not a surprise to God. He knows exactly where you are. His desire is that you join Him in every facet of your life. When you join Him, whether you're happy or sad, your emotional state becomes God's territory. Your desires must be embedded in the will of God. Psalm 37:4–5 says, "Delight yourself also in the Lord; and He shall give you the desires of your heart. Commit your way to the Lord, trust also in Him, and He shall bring it to pass."

We learn the will of God through a process; and just as time itself cannot be hurried, we cannot rush the learning process. God provides us with many indicators of His very character, one of which we see in the grandeur of the seasons. They move along from one to the other in a splendor that humbles our very souls before Him. The wealthier one is, the less important it is to prove their net worth. God owns everything. We are simply stewards of His wealth. When we die, we will take nothing tangible with us. So as stewards, we are to recognize that since God owns it all, we are simply entrusted with a portion of it. In other words, God sets us up in a heavenly business, gives us the success manual, and expects positive results. It is perhaps the only business deal initiated and overseen by pure love.

A great example of our being placed in business by the Lord begins in Matthew 25:14 where Jesus explains that a man of means left for a far country. This man had others (servants) working for him. He gave one servant five talents, another servant two, and another one. He knew their abilities and, therefore, gave each accordingly. The intent of the owner was that the servants would do their best with what he had entrusted them. After a long time, the owner returned and called for an accounting. The first two servants had doubled their employer's money, but the third had done nothing but bury the money in the ground. The first two servants were rewarded with great promotions, while the third was called wicked and lazy. The third servant was fired and cast out because he had done nothing with what he had been given.

James 1:17 tells us that "Every good gift and every perfect gift is from above, and comes down from the Father of lights." Wealth is one of those gifts from above, and we are to view it as such. Gifts are not worked for. But you say, "God gave us a brain, and we are to use it." That's a true statement; however, our brain cannot be responsible for adding one day to our lives nor adding a single penny to our bank account. We are simply to use our brain power to search for the avenues to multiply the gifts we have been given.

We show our Christian maturity, or lack thereof, when it comes to money. It is very easy to get out of balance in this area. When we cross the line in our attempts to gain more, the scripture faithfully issues a warning, as in 1 Timothy 6:9–10: "Those who desire to be rich fall into temptation and a snare, and into many foolish and harmful lusts which drown men in destruction and perdition. For the love of money is a root of all kinds of evil, for which some have strayed from the faith in their greediness, and pierced themselves through with many sorrows." Our love must be in the source of the money and not in the money itself.

Being part of the kingdom of God is a wonderful privilege and responsibility, but it must always be lived in humility and in the spirit of a true servant. The *Holman Bible Dictionary* describes humility as a personal quality by which an individual shows dependence on God and respect for other persons. Matthew 23:11 says, "But He who is greatest among you shall be your servant." We are to emulate Christ who lived His life in service to others while on earth. We are to use our God-given talents and gifts to His glory, and He will multiply our bounty as we serve Him.

Once we buy into the truth that our maximum blessings result from a life totally yielded to God, through Christ, things begin falling into place for our good. We understand that God will always be at the head of everything and that "all things work together for good to those who love God, to those who are the called according to His purpose" (Romans 8:28).

With your list that answers the three questions (1. Where am I? 2. Where do I want to go? and 3. How will I get there?), determine today that you will seek to achieve these desires of your heart as you "Delight yourself also in the Lord" (Psalm 37:4). Adopt Romans 13:8 as your very own motto in the area of finance: "Owe no one anything except to love one another." Get out of debt!

No matter your financial condition, begin tithing to the Lord. Although God owns 100 percent of our incomes, He commands us to be faithful to return to Him 10 percent of it. This is a necessary exercise to test our accountability as a steward or faithful servant. But you say, "I can't afford it. I don't have the money." Do what is right. Malachi 3:10 says to "Bring all the tithes into the storehouse, that there may be food in My house, and try Me now in this, says the Lord of hosts, if I will not open for you the windows of heaven and pour out for you such blessing that there will not be room enough to receive it." Try it. It works!

Very few people today are financially free. Be one of the few! Trust the Lord and obey His Word, and this freedom will happen. The gift of God lives in us through the power of the Holy Spirit.

Whatever comes our way, "We have this treasure in earthen vessels that the excellence of the power may be of God, and not of us. We are hard-pressed on every side, yet not crushed; we are perplexed, but not in despair; persecuted, but not forsaken; struck down, but not destroyed" (2 Corinthians 4:7–9).

God gives us the power to live on the high plane of freedom from worldly bondage, but we must obey the manual (Bible). He assures us in Luke 12:31 that He knows what we need, but we are to "seek the kingdom of God; and all these things shall be added to [us]." He reminds us that "Where your treasure is, there your heart will be also" (Luke 12:34). Make sure your treasure is in Him.

Learning to live our lives God's way will bring everything we could ever hope for. Then at the end of this life, we will have built treasures in heaven.

The wealthiest day of our lives will be at the judgment seat of Christ when we are judged righteous and enter into heaven. Nothing will be more important than that moment.

Actively Waiting

Actively waiting can best be pictured in the planning of a formal wedding. The date is set, and the wait is on. Yet, this is one of the busiest times in the lives of the prospective bride and groom. Christ compares the church to a bride and Himself to the groom. When He was crucified on the cross, he paid the dowry required by God the Father. This payment was in the giving of His life for the church.

In Jewish history, the betrothal ceremony marked the beginning of the engagement period. It was a serious occasion, as only a written divorce could break the engagement. Divorce was granted only because of death or sexual infidelity. Christ told the disciples during their three-year ministry together that He would leave them, go to heaven where He would prepare a place for them and the rest of the church, and then return to claim His bride and take her to heaven to be forever with Him (John 14). Since the time of His ascension, the wait has been on. But there is much to be done.

The parable of the ten virgins in Matthew 25 is a simple story that stresses the importance of being prepared for the coming of the Lord, our groom. All the virgins had the necessary equipment (the lamps), but only five of them had made ample provision for the waiting. Since the oil in the lamps was the source of the lamp's light, could it be that Christ is comparing Christians to lamps (vessels) and

Himself to the oil (the source of the light)? As holy vessels of light, we must be continually filled with the oil of the Holy Spirit.

Each of the virgins knew that the bridegroom would return for her, but none knew when he would return. All simply were aware of the importance of being prepared. The preparation in this story was that of having lamps with ample oil on hand to insure a continual flame.

At midnight, a thunderous announcement proclaimed that the bridegroom was coming, and the invitation went out for his bride to come and join him. The virgins excitedly awoke from their rest, and five of them quickly began trimming their lamps as they filled them to capacity with oil. The remaining five's lamps had gone out, and they had brought no oil with them. They all knew that in order to be invited into the marriage, they must be prepared with lighted lamps. The wise virgins could not afford to share their oil at that late date and risk their lamps going out, so they advised the foolish virgins to go and buy more from the distributor. The foolish virgins had no other choice but to hurry off in a scramble; but while they were gone, the bridegroom came and took those prepared into the marriage; and the door was shut.

Two thousand years have passed since Christ's resurrection, but the command for preparation is as alive today as it was when He first spoke it through the Word. He continues to abide in human tabernacles, our bodies (Revelation 21:3), and He does not change (Malachi 3:6).

The Scripture tells us beginning at 2 Peter 3:3, "Scoffers will come in the last days, walking according to their own lusts, and saying, 'Where is the promise of His coming? For since the fathers fell asleep, all things continue as they were from the beginning of creation.'" We are then told in verses 8 and following, "Beloved, do not forget this one thing, that with the Lord one day is as a thousand years, and a thousand years as one day. The Lord is not slack concerning His promise, as some count slackness, but is longsuffering toward us, not willing that any should perish but that all should come to repentance. But the day of the Lord will come as a thief in the night."

Generations come and go, but few leave this world fully prepared. Ephesians 5:14–15 tells us to "Awake, you who sleep, arise from the dead, and Christ will give you light. See then that you walk circumspectly, not as fools but as wise."

The Bible is full of simple stories (parables) that make little sense apart from interpretation by the Holy Spirit. The disciples of Christ asked Him in Matthew 13:10, "Why do You speak to them in parables?" His answer came in verse 11: "Because it is given to you to know the mysteries of the kingdom of heaven, but to them it has not been given." Understanding the Bible could only be done through Christ while He was on earth and through the teaching of the Holy Spirit since His resurrection.

One parable was so very important to Christ that it is recorded three times in the gospels: Matthew 13, Mark 4, and Luke 8. It tells the story of a sower sowing seeds and the types of ground on which they were sown. Some fell by the wayside where they were trampled and the birds ate them. Some fell upon a rock where they withered away because they lacked moisture. Some fell among thorns where the seeds were choked out when the thorns grew. But other seeds fell on good ground where they grew and produced a great yield. The disciples asked for the meaning of the parable.

The understanding was very simple although it had seemed almost a riddle or mystery before Christ's interpretation. Christ explained that the seed is the Word of God. Those by the wayside are those who hear; then the devil comes and takes the Word out of their hearts, lest they should believe and be saved. Those on the rock are ones who, when they hear, receive the Word with joy and, for a time, believe, but, having no root, fall away in time of temptation. The seeds which fall among thorns are those who, when they have heard, go forth but are choked with the cares and riches and pleasures of this life and bring no fruit to perfection. But the seeds that are sown in the good ground are those who, with an honest and good heart, hear the Word, keep it, and bring forth fruit with patience.

Many good-intentioned people think that they will be eternally saved because they once were in a church service and believed what was being said. Yet, the parable says there is more to salvation than that. The Word must penetrate the heart that honestly wants to receive it; and then the Bible (Word) becomes the guide book for those who have heard and received it, thereby fulfilling the requirements of salvation. Don't be deceived; salvation is not simply mental ascent that God is in heaven and the Bible is true. It must become a part of you to where it motivates your very life and purpose.

Let's put it another way. In John 15:1, Christ compares our relationship with Him as that of Him being a vine and us being branches. Through guidance and correction by obeying the Word, we become clean and produce that which God intends for our lives. As a branch cannot live without the vine, we cannot live (eternally) without total dependence on the vine, Christ, the Giver of life. In John 15:5, Christ says we can do nothing except through Him. What does this mean? To most people, if we can pay our bills and have money left over, then we think we are really "something." To God, unless we accept Christ as our personal Savior and Lord, we are accounted as doing "nothing" before Him. He desires that first we make a personal decision that will carry us to and through eternity with Him. This life is only a speck on the time line. Our Groom has gone to heaven and is preparing a place for His bride, the church. We are to be ever mindful of the fact that He will return, so it is vital that we be prepared. We abide in Him by being committed to Him and His Word.

A promise that is sure to get our attention is in John 15:7: "If you abide in Me, and My words abide in you, you will ask what you desire, and it shall be done for you." That statement contains a lot of wisdom. If we are abiding in Him and He is abiding in us, we will only ask those things that are in His will for us.

The parable of the vine and branches paints a picture of an intimate relationship in which we cannot survive victoriously without total dependence on the source of life. Until we grasp this truth, distractions accumulate and dominate our lives. Life circumstances can become one huge distraction. If allowed, they will dominate our lives to the point that we live by *reacting* rather than acting. Victory comes at the most unexpected times, at those times when life has become so burdened and weighted that at our lowest point we come to the end of self-effort and look up and receive a refreshing new life that was God's gift and plan all along.

In radically releasing our lives to the purpose of God, much waiting will occur along the way. We do not like waiting. It seems that nothing happens when we wait. But the truth is that more happens while we wait than we would acknowledge. Waiting is generally unwelcome. Yet through waiting, character builds traits of love, joy, peace, patience, gentleness, goodness, faithfulness, meekness, and temperance. These are the fruit of the Spirit of God which we do not want to miss!

Much of living is spent in the waiting line. Think of what could be accomplished if we took advantage of this time; for example, waiting in traffic could be times of prayerful solitude, waiting for news that would assuredly affect our lives could be spent in confirming our trust in God through meditation and prayer, etc. Waiting could be times of strengthening the foundations of our lives. Obedient waiting ushers in spiritual progress unparalleled to anything imaginable in the physical.

As we wait for the inevitable return of Christ, take advantage of the wait. Like the ten virgins, we have one responsibility, and that is to be prepared. Being that good ground in which God's Word is planted is paramount for living powerfully in Christ. Abiding or resting in total dependence on the Lord is a must. Do not allow life to pass you by without active waiting. Don't be caught off guard. Be wise.

Walk the Talk

In today's world system, anyone with a platform from which to speak is often perceived as an expert. When we hear their thoughts over and over again, the more believable they become, and we soon accept them as truth. The fact is that this kind of "truth," apart from the source of truth, is error and leads to inevitable bondage and defeat. Breaking free from this gullible mind-set is simple but not easy. It is a sober choice. Romans 8:22 speaks of the whole creation groaning as in the pains of childbirth. Overall, this world is tired and in much pain. Thankfully, however, deliverance is available for all who sincerely desire it.

Day-to-day living becomes your walk in life, and your ideals (a conception of something in its absolute perfection) become your talk. It is easy to present an idealistic picture when giving advice to others, but the challenge is to apply those same ideals to our own lives to the point that they become *our* walk or way of life. For ideals to become true reality, there is but one source to turn to, and that is to the truth, the Bible.

Jeremiah 17:9 says, "The heart is deceitful above all things, and desperately wicked." We cannot trust our own judgments apart from God, as without Him we walk in what the Bible calls the flesh. Walking in the flesh brings about conflict and war because no common denominator serves as a guide. God's Word is the guide. Proverbs 17:28 shows how looks are deceiving when it says that "Even a fool is counted wise when he holds his peace; when he shuts his lips, he is considered perceptive."

James 1:25 tells us that "He who looks into the perfect law of liberty (the Bible) and continues in it, and is not a forgetful hearer but a doer of the work, this one will be blessed in what he does." Therefore, we must be single focused, making the main thing the main thing. So how can we do this without coming across as a fanatic or weirdo?

If you haven't by this time accepted Jesus Christ as your personal Savior and Lord, the Messiah, you owe it to yourself to read the Bible for validity of its truth. Before beginning to read, be bold enough to pray to the God whom you do not yet know, that if He is really there, to make Himself known to you. Seek the truth with all that is in you. This is an important exclusive time toward filling a most critical void in your life. You will be awed by a new rock-solid strength resultant from these days of reading. You will also appreciate the Bible as not just another good book. And you will look no more a fanatic or weirdo than you were before!

If you are already a Christian, your victory is in the pages of the Bible. Many Christians walk in defeat because they do not take advantage of reading and learning the wisdom and direction it provides. You cannot simply talk about God's way, read good books about it, or depend solely on the church to teach you. You must study the Bible as God's personal Word to you. Psalm 119:105 says, "Your Word is a lamp to my feet and a light to my path." As you walk through the Word and apply it, it becomes your talk.

As you begin this new walk of consistently reading the Bible for either proof of its validity or godly success in living, examine it carefully. This is a serious time in your life where you are quietly determining truth that will turn the course of your life here on earth to purpose as well as affirm your assurance of living eternally in the kingdom of God. This is a time to discover and solidify your beliefs.

Firstly, begin your journey in Proverbs. There are thirty-one chapters in the book of Proverbs. For each day of the month, select the chapter for that day and read it as if it were instructions to you personally. It truly is! For example, if you begin this process of reading on the thirtieth of the month, then read Proverbs 30 on that day. This is a great book for practical living. Test what it says against your perception of truth. Highlight those areas that are particularly meaningful to you.

Secondly, begin reading the book of Psalms; but, beforehand, decide on the time of day that is most convenient for your reading. Set a maximum time for reading. Fifteen- to thirty-minute intervals are good time slots. Timing might vary from day to day, and perhaps now is the time to begin scheduling other activities in your day as well. By scheduling your time, you will effectively accomplish daily tasks that you only talked about before.

The Psalms will encourage you as you begin realizing the freedom, joy, and peace that you gain only through scripture reading. This book is full of emotion that will build a strong sense of faith. Again, read as if the book were written directly to you and for you. And truly it is!

After completing the Psalms, begin in the New Testament at the gospel of John. This book will introduce you to Christ in His deity as the Son of God. Ask God continually for understanding of what you are reading. Highlight all meaningful verses. Take your time as you read. Continue reading through the New Testament to the end of Revelation in short daily intervals. There will be much that you will not understand; but by the help of the Holy Spirit, you will understand enough.

Next, read Matthew, Mark, and Luke. These books, along with John, portray the life of Christ in multifaceted ways. On completion, you will have read the entire New Testament and developed a unique relationship with the King of kings and Lord of lords.

Now, you will be ready to officially start at the beginnings, Genesis. Read straight through the Old Testament. As you read, look for all references to Christ, the Messiah. These Old Testament books were written hundreds of years before the birth of Christ, but the exactness of the details of fulfilled prophesy cannot be denied. They are history. Some of the Old Testament books are labor intensive, but plow through them, as you will learn to appreciate the importance our Jehovah God places on every single person, place, and thing. In this difficult reading, return to books you read in the Psalms and the New Testament that have encouraged you. Read and reread each day in Proverbs. The wisdom in these chapters will help you tremendously in your daily living. Proverbs 2:7–8 says, "He (God) stores up sound wisdom for the upright; He is a shield to those who walk uprightly; He guards the paths of justice and preserves the way of His saints."

Bible reading is indeed spiritual food. Reading the Bible is different from reading any other book. It is not for speed reading—it is a manual of instruction for successfully living God's way. Read it for discernment on living and walking through this life with purpose.

Those with economic status and mental brilliance, winners and losers, all stand on level ground before their Almighty Creator. God allows us such freedom that even before we come to know Him, we are allowed to think we are in control of the success or failure in our lives—that it's all up to us. Nothing could be farther from the truth.

Though God is the great *I AM*—the all in all to everything from eternity past to eternity future—Psalm 103:13–14 assures us that "As a father pities (shows compassion for) his children, so the Lord pities those who fear (reverence) Him; for He knows our frame,

He remembers that we are dust." The strongest among us is weak compared to our Father God. He is high and holy, continually ruling in love with an open hand.

God is the originator of natural laws, and these laws will not and cannot be broken or changed. He speaks clearly in Malachi 3:6: "For I am the Lord, I do not change." Every principle in scripture from Genesis to Revelation is set and is unchangeable. Our lives become messed up by repeated poor decisions that are in violation of the Scriptures. Most bad decisions are made, not because of willful intent, but because of ignorance due to lack of knowledge of the Word (Hosea 4:6).

The Bible rests on dusty shelves with its pages rustling with life, but we will not know *that life* unless we receive and apply it. Just because mankind does not read or honor the Word does not mean that it is dead or nonexistent. It is as much alive, true, and in the heart of God now as it was when He prompted men to write it on parchment.

Once you understand the importance of accepting the scriptural truths that you do not actually control the events in your walk (life) and that your only responsibility is to strive to be blameless before God, then you will be well on your way to joining Him in your quest. You are then relieved of life's burdens that were not intended at all for you.

Walking the talk does not come naturally. The goal of the walk is perfection that we can achieve only as we walk in the footsteps and the shadow of the Lord through His Word. But you say, "No one is perfect." In and of us, that is a correct statement. Yet it is not about us. We are simply to receive the gift that will cover us in perfection. The gift is that of receiving Jesus Christ as our salvation. It is what He did in submission and dying on the cross as a sacrifice for all sin that we are declared righteous and perfect.

Because of a trick of the devil, many Christians fall into the guilt of believing that we must do good deeds to keep our salvation fires burning and secure. As a natural birth cannot be undone, neither can a spiritual birth. If you ever truly accept, believe, and confess Jesus Christ as your Savior and Lord, you will be born again, and you cannot be unborn. Works become the by-product of obedience by the prompting of the Holy Spirit through the reading of the Bible. It is very important to read and understand God's Word for yourself, as heresy abounds everywhere in this world, even from some of our church pulpits.

Be proactive in obedience to what you are reading in the Bible. But don't think you will do everything exactly right. Radical perfecting results from a continual reading of the Word and acting on its truth. Always remember that only one sinless person ever walked the face of the earth, and He was Jesus Christ, God in flesh. As Isaiah 53 has prophesied hundreds of years before His birth, Jesus would not be recognized by the world. That's why worldly wisdom is of no eternal value.

1 John 5:19–20 encourages believers by saying, "We know that we are of God, and the whole world lies under the sway of the wicked one. And we know that the Son of God has come and has given us an understanding, that we may know Him who is true; and we are in Him who is true, in His Son Jesus Christ. This is the true God and eternal life." We must attach ourselves to the One who controls our eternity.

As your godly wisdom increases, your old goals and desires will fade as you take on new zeal and direction. Don't rush ahead of God. Simply keep reading and praying for His talk (the Bible) to be your walk.

Submitted and Free

In the core of every human being is a longing to be free. But freedom does not just happen. Conditions must be met and practiced in order that any measure of it can be enjoyed. The first of the Ten Commandments (Exodus 20:3) emphatically instructs us to have no other gods before Jehovah God. That theme runs with profound subtlety throughout the entirety of the Bible. God takes second place to nothing or to no one else. But since He operates in the spiritual realm in the highest form of love, mercy, and holiness, it is very difficult for us, in this tangible world, to take hold of the reality that God is also the master Controller over this world and He makes Himself known only as we freely respond and submit to His plan.

God's plan contains no bondage, only total freedom. When you make your "life decision" to receive Jesus Christ into your total being, you will experience your first major release from bondage: a release from the fear of death and hell that was a certainty beforehand. You will have just been "born again" (John 3:3). Just as you were born of the flesh into this physical life, you must be born of the Spirit in order to enter into the kingdom of God (John 3:5).

Real freedom, the God kind of freedom, produces ecstasy as we move purposefully through the journey of life. In radically releasing ourselves into submission to God, in Christ, and abiding in the

Word through the instruction of His Holy Spirit, we soon learn that life on earth is simply the starting line. 1 Corinthians 13:12 tells us that "Now we see in a mirror, dimly, but then face to face. Now I know in part, but then I shall know just as I also am known." Sin is so predominate in this world that it shrouds us in every way, including our vision. It is purely by submitting to the power of God that we are made free from such sin.

From the model prayer, "Your will be done on earth as it is in heaven" (Matthew 6:10), we become aware that heaven blesses anything done in obedience to Christ, the Word. Living free is living submitted to God through His Word. That very blessing joins heaven to earth.

Now here we are, free from the penalty of sin forever, but still tied in the bondage of complicated life circumstances. Only One, God the Father, can unscramble the impossible. That's His business! Luke 1:37 assures us that "With God nothing will be impossible." God knew us before we were born, whether born in the lap of luxury or in the pit of squalor (Psalm 139). In His economy, we all stand equally before Him, housed with potential that can make us free only as we discover and submit to Him.

Immeasurable benefits await all who totally submit to the Lord. We become aware that nothing happens outside His control. If we are wrapped up in Him, nothing can harm us. 1 Peter 3:12 says, "For the eyes of the Lord are on the righteous and His ears are open to their prayers; but the face of the Lord is against those who do evil." When we are submitted to the King of kings, we are sealed in His purpose and plan.

But you say, "What about those who have faced unprecedented torture and martyrdom for their faith?" Be assured that those precious saints walked from this life into the next with full assurance of Psalm 116:15: "Precious in the sight of the Lord is the death of His saints." For the Christian, we have nothing to fear because we strengthen our faith by continuing to absorb Scripture into our hearts through reading, preaching, and teaching. Most will never be required to face martyrdom; but for those who are, God has a blessing awaiting them worth the sacrifice.

Ecclesiastes 3:2 assures us that we all have "a time to be born and a time to die." We cannot escape death; it is out of our hands; but we can be prepared. We have all witnessed catastrophic events where no one should have lived, but did. At other times, a simple bump to the head resulted in death. Indeed, God is the master Controller.

[handwritten left margin: WE CANNOT ESCAPE DEATH BUT WE CAN BE PREPARED]

Intellectually, we all desire the best for ourselves and make efforts to achieve that best. Most of this effort, however, is for the here and now and does not go beyond this life. Intellectual acknowledgment that there is a God in heaven will not take us there. We must submit to God through the blood sacrifice of Christ. There is no other way. If voices in your head are telling you to forget this book because of its radical nature, simply denounce those voices. One day when the darkness of sin has been lifted from this world and after God finally flings Satan and all his followers into everlasting torment, you will be glad that you submitted. If you find this scary, it is! But it's better scary than lost forever don't you think?

From the beginning of this book to now, you have received awakening news of the urgency of joining yourself to God in Christ and becoming part of the living church of God. It is not a mental exercise; it is a relationship that will carry you on the wings of the Almighty to the heights of blessed living. Just as you can never enjoy a nice swim without jumping into the deep and becoming immersed in the very vehicle that will allow you freedom to move, you must radically release yourself into the depths of Scripture for real freedom, not only for the here and now but forever.

When you begin your new life, you will be different. Your ideals will have changed. However, although your heart and mind desire the things of God, you must yield every day of your life to Him in order to achieve the success He intends for you.

Romans 6:16 says, "Do you not know that to whom you present yourselves slaves to obey, you are that one's slaves whom you obey, whether of sin leading to death, or of obedience leading to righteousness?" Even with your name in the Lamb's Book of life, you are still living in a sinful world; and you will always be tempted with choices that could move you into defeat. As you awaken to the fact that you are living in a wicked, uncaring world, it will make you sad even to the point of tears; but your sorrow will be turned into joy one day (John 16:20). If you are a Christian, rejoice. Grow in your day-to-day wisdom as you read and meditate on the scriptures and pray. Search for your true purpose that will lead to completeness as you live your life. You will be greatly rewarded.

Does victory come immediately? Yes, in part. Salvation is your first major step to a freedom that brings unexplainable assurance and rest to the heart and soul. The next step in your victory journey is that of reading the "Map" for personal direction. Follow its instructions—it is your ticket to deliverance onto the road that God has preplanned for you. Life will become one of adventure.

Although your future is secure, be aware that the "old foe" will wake up. It will alarm him that he has lost one of his own to the other side. He will do everything possible, by anyone possible, to get you back. You must give every evil thought and action over to your Deliverer. You can rest in the assurance that He can handle them all. Submission will take practice, as you are new at the game; and it will seem to be a natural to try to fight life's battles your old way. Your fight is in learning to believe God. That is true faith.

Go to church. In doing so, you will be joined by others of like minds. Learn from what is taught in church, but be sure that what is being taught agrees with the daily Scriptures you are reading. Give of yourself, your time, and your money as you are prompted and instructed by the Holy Spirit and the Bible. Be patient as you live with and around others. Everyone is on a different level of spiritual maturity, and your marker for treating others is as you would want to be treated. *DO UNTO OTHERS . . .*

Do your part toward applying good health principles and trust God to provide your heart's desires. Wait on the Lord as you live a clean life before Him. Trust Him in your daily living that He will work all things for your good because He "has saved us and called us with a holy calling, not according to our works, but according to His own purpose and grace which was given to us in Christ Jesus before time began" (2 Timothy 1:9). As you live in obedience to the Lord, you will see a gradual change in your life that will move you toward realizing goals and desires that were before only far-off dreams.

Christ in God is King of kings and Lord of lords; and as children of the King, we are then heirs—heirs of God and joint heirs with Christ (Romans 8:16–17). We are to take our place in our Father's royal kingdom here on earth and live in submission to the rules of the kingdom (the Bible). Children of earthly kings are taught from birth a certain protocol. It becomes the only accepted way of life for them. God's kingdom is no different. We, as God's children, are royalty; and we should live to bring honor to His kingdom. We soon learn that submission brings total freedom that continues into eternity. Wow! What a future we have! "Even so, come, Lord Jesus!" (Revelation 22:20).

TO HIM SUBMISSION BRINGS TOTAL FREEDOM THAT CONTINUES INTO ETERNITY

Closing Prayer

O God, in Jesus's name, I pray for those who are drawn to the words in this book. I pray that they will use it as a guide to point them to truth for their lives. I pray that they will be freed from insecurity, defeat, emptiness, anger, bitterness, guilt, depression, anxiety, failure, boredom, and poverty. I pray that their hearts and lives will be filled with love, joy, peace, patience, happiness, success, and prosperity. Make them new, oh Lord of heaven. Engulf them with Your presence.

Lord, as I reflect in these sunset years, thank You for my life experiences, both good and bad. The good times were encouragements to me. The bad times have proven better, as they compelled me to reach outside myself to You. Oh, thank You for the bad times. Today I am strong, not in myself, but in You because I have learned that in the very act of accepting You as my Lord and God, nothing or no one can harm me. I am sealed to the day of redemption.

Thank You, Lord, for teaching me that my own strength is no strength at all, but Your strength in me can move mountains. Thank You for teaching me that within myself, I have no rights, but in You I have every right. Thank You for freedom in a world that is imprisoned. Oh, thank You, Lord!

Amen and Amen.   GOD BLESS YOU, GLORIA,
          10-6-19   AND THANK
                              YOU FOR
                              THIS LITTLE
                              BOOK ♡

About the Author

Gloria Poage, a Christian neighbor next door, has lived and worked in the business world for years, is active in the local church, and is a proclaimer of the truth of the Word of God to all the world through her strong communication skills. Her message is that of "Yes and Amen" in our Lord Jesus Christ, God the Son.

CPSIA information can be obtained
at www.ICGtesting.com
Printed in the USA
FSHW012308160719
60039FS